Ghosts

of the

Ghostlight Theatre

Told to you by Starry Night Theatre's cast, crew, and audience members past and present

Compiled by Amanda R. Woomer
Foreword by L. Don Swartz

In memory of the players who have gone on before us:

Carl Tamburlin
Jedidiah Woomer
Stephen Holesko
John Kerr

Other books from Spook-Eats by Amanda R. Woomer:

A Haunted Atlas of Western New York:
a Spooky Guide to the Strange and Unusual

THE SPIRIT GUIDE:
America's Haunted Breweries, Distilleries, and
Wineries

Creepy Books for Creepy Kids:

The Cryptid ABC Book

Krampus's Great Big Book of Yuletide Monsters

Contents

Foreword

Amanda and I met at the Ghostlight Theatre many years ago and immediately bonded over our shared love of all things ghostly! We have worked on countless theatrical productions together and have enjoyed multiple ghost hunts. For years, we talked about compiling the many ghost stories at the Ghostlight Theatre, and Amanda has finally done it!

As the owner of Spook-Eats and author of many wonderful books on the supernatural, I knew our stories were in the most capable hands. What I wasn't prepared for was the impact the stories would have on me.

Amanda has compiled the recollection of over 45 people who have had (sometimes multiple) supernatural experiences at the Ghostlight Theatre. She has assembled these stories in such a clear and concise manner so as to allow each individual voice to be heard. As I read these eye witness accounts in each person's unique voice, I found myself getting very emotional. These people were sharing a deeply personal experience that they had while in the theatre, and many of the stories cut right to the heart. I knew the stories would scare me. I did not realize how deeply some of the recollections would touch me.

What Amanda has done with this book is quite remarkable. She has created a literary collage of eyewitness accounts in such a way as to place the reader smack dab inside the Ghostlight Theatre. The principal character is the building itself. As the stories unfold, it is the theatre itself that comes to life!

How she managed that, I have no idea. What I do know is that you are going to love the adventure she is about to send you on.

L. Don Swartz
Just another writer

Introduction

Any respectable theatre has at least one good ghost story. Why should the Ghostlight Theatre be any different? After all, it's one of the oldest theatres in all of Western New York, having been built decades before the Riviera Theatre, the Rapids Theatre, and Shea's Performing Arts Center (all of which are also haunted).

The Ghostlight Theatre has stood in the heart of North Tonawanda for over a century, initially as a church and, most recently, as the home of Starry Night Theatre, Inc.

Over the years, hundreds and thousands of people have walked across the Ghostlight Theatre's threshold and have been transported to places like Castle Dracula and introduced to some interesting characters like Lottie and Bernice.

And when people come and go over the years, they sometimes leave memories and imprints in their wake.

Theatres are some of the most haunted places on the planet. But why? Could the performing arts—something that actors pour their hearts and souls into—reach across time and space and leave a lasting impression on a location? Could the laughter, tears, and screams from an audience fuel the energy of the actors on stage and the building as well? Could period pieces set in the 19th Century like *A Christmas Carol* or *The Lodger* attract spirits searching for a bit of familiarity? Perhaps.

Throw in electrical equipment (thought to stir up the supernatural) like lightbulbs, extension cords, soundboards, and computers used for each production, and you have a veritable buffet for the paranormal.

Starry Night Theatre, Inc. has called the Ghostlight Theatre its home for 20 years now (come January 2021). And while you might not see our beloved theatre featured on ghost hunting shows on TV, for many of us—cast, crew, and even loyal audience members—the Ghostlight is one of the most haunted places we've ever been.

We'd like to share our stories with you… that is… if you're not too scared.

-a.r.w.

About Spook-Eats

Spook-Eats is a travel website where we visit haunted restaurants, bars, and hotels, trying the food, telling the ghost stories, and searching for spirits of all kinds.

To learn more about Spook-Eats, you can find us on Facebook, Instagram, and Twitter, as well as our website www.spookeats.com.

An Important Note

Spook-Eats and the author of this book do not support or endorse trespassing to any haunted locations, including the Ghostlight Theatre. Before visiting the Ghostlight Theatre, make sure you obtain the proper permission, visit during business hours, attend a performance with a ticket, honor signs that designate cast and crew only locations, and/or book a ghost tour with us.

Happy haunting!

Theatre & Paranormal Vocabulary

You'll find that many of these ghost stories include theatre vocabulary that you may be unfamiliar with. To give you the best understanding of our tales and our building, get to know these common theatre and paranormal terms:

Center Stage: the middle of the stage.

Cue: anything said or done on/offstage that is followed by a specific action such as a sound or an entrance.

EMF: electromagnetic field. An area produced by moving electrical charges. Generally not paranormal. However, when there are no electrical sources, it may be considered paranormal.

EVP: electronic voice phenomena. Spirit voices caught on electrical equipment such as digital recorders and cameras.

Ghost Light: a light that is always left on in theatres when the building is dark and empty. Some say it is to appease the spirits and offer them a chance to perform on stage, while others claim it is to keep the ghosts away. Most theatres have a ghost light.

Green Room: the backstage waiting area for actors before, during, and after a performance. Not necessarily green.

House: the auditorium where the audience sits.

House Left: the left-hand side when you're looking at the stage.

House Right: the right-hand side when you're looking at the stage.

Residual Energy: remnants of energy that can be left in a location or an object. Not considered "intelligent" but rather a moment playing on repeat.

Stage Left: the left-hand side when you're standing on the stage.

Stage Right: the right-hand side when you're standing on the stage.

The

Ghosts

of the

Ghostlight Theatre

Told to you by Starry Night Theatre's cast, crew, and audience members past and present

Compiled by Amanda R. Woomer
Foreword by L. Don Swartz

A Brief History of the Ghostlight Theatre

The Ghostlight Theatre was not always the home of Starry Night Theatre, Inc. Up until 2001, it was the home of the Evangelical Friedens Church of North Tonawanda.

According to legend, the church's cornerstone was laid on a dark and stormy Halloween night in 1889. Supposedly, a need for this new church arrived when the Erie Canal separated Tonawanda and North Tonawanda, cutting off a small group of German immigrants from the rest of their congregation. After years of little help from their Synod, the North Tonawanda members decided to splinter off and formed their own church. They were called the Deutsche Vereinigte Evangelische Friedens Gemeinde (or the German United Evangelical Peace Congregation) of North Tonawanda.

The Friedens Church was a part of the North Tonawanda community, standing tall (with its 80-foot steeple) on the corners of Schenck and Vandervoort for

1

over 110 years until the building was given to L. Don Swartz and it was renamed the Ghostlight Theatre.

Since Starry Night Theatre, Inc. moved into the old church, volunteers both on stage and off have reported  unusual and unexplained activity throughout the building from the "Early America" room in the basement, to the costume room on the second floor, in the prop room backstage, and up in the balcony. The most haunted place in the entire theatre is believed to be the infamous spiral staircase. There, EVPs have been captured saying people's names, the sound of phantom footsteps have been heard, and most who venture up the stairs share a feeling of uneasiness.

Over the years, several paranormal teams have investigated the theatre, including Soul Seekers United, Western New York Paranormal, Erie County Paranormal Association, and Buffalo Paranormal Society. Most recently, the building was featured on Joe Pieri's solo investigation with Paranormal Crossroads on Paranormal Warehouse and will be featured in an upcoming documentary.

Supposedly, several spirits are haunting the old church now turned theatre, the most famous of them being the Lady in Red. No one knows who she is or why she still lingers at the Ghostlight Theatre, but the Lady in Red is known to appear to volunteers as a full-bodied apparition, seeming so life-like that people don't realize who (or rather, what) she is until she's gone.

Aside from full-bodied apparitions (though that is impressive in and of itself), the Ghostlight Theatre's spirits have made themselves known by running around and moving hangers in the costume room, through electronic recordings (spoken in both English and German), as well as appearing in photographs.

In recent years, the theatre has opened its doors to guests for their ghost hunt evenings, offering amateur paranormal investigators the chance to explore parts of the theatre usually off-limits to guests—including the bell tower where the 2,800-pound bell still hangs.

The Ghostlight Theatre seems to be almost alive with spirits coming and going as they please. Some are from over a century ago, and others only departed this world within the last few years. No matter when or where they're from, it is clear that their presence is felt throughout the theatre, as they silently watch the performers on stage (and sometimes even make a cameo).

The Evangelical Friedens Church is seen on the corners of
Schenck and Vandervoort with the parsonage next door. While
these two buildings are still standing, the neighborhood looks very
different in the 21st Century.

A snapshot from the Friedens Church's Old Maid's Convention
from 1908.

The church circa 1930
vs.
The theatre 2020

"Friendly Visitation Sunday" on September 25, 1927.
This is the front porch that patrons enter through to access the box
office and theatre today.

The view from the balcony circa 1930 vs. 2020

A snapshot from Vacation Bible School in the 1920-1930s. While the clothes may not match her description, two women who have seen the Lady in Red claim this woman is who they saw.

The Hot Spots

Over the years, many cast and crew members have picked up on certain areas scattered throughout the theatre that they prefer to avoid if they can (especially if they're alone). Even audience members and people who are visiting for the first time occasionally feel uneasy near these areas.

While most people agree that there is nothing malicious lurking in the Ghostlight Theatre, everyone tends to acknowledge that there are five places hidden in the theatre where the energy feels a bit "off."

You'll find that many of the accounts from cast, crew, and audience members focus on these areas of the theatre.

Hot Spot #1:
The Hall Leading to the Office

If you've attended a show and wandered down into the basement during intermission, then you know this hallway quite well.

As you walk along the hall (usually packed with people buying snacks or 50/50 tickets), you'll pass what many at the Ghostlight call the "Early America" room filled with photos from past productions. You'll also walk

by the concession stand and the kitchen area only to be greeted by a dead end with a drinking fountain and the theatre's office.

This small section of the theatre has made people uneasy for years. It could be because the large art gallery is at your back or passing by doorways into the "Early

America" room and the kitchen suddenly makes you feel vulnerable… that, and basements just tend to be scary in general.

Hot Spot #2:
The Stairs Leading to the Costume Room

It's an area most audience members don't see, but cast and crew will constantly be running up and down these stairs during a performance, all while trying to not think about where they are.

Located stage right, these stairs run from the green room up past several secret entrances to the stage and end at the costume room.

For many, the costume room stairs are the first place they feel uneasy in the theatre. With the number of stories surrounding these stairs (and the costume room, itself), it's no surprise that the innocent looking stairs are yet another paranormal hot spot in the theatre.

Hot Spot #3:

The Basement Storage Area

You may not notice at first when you're lingering in the art gallery in the basement, but you're surrounded by hidden storage areas.

As you make your way down the flight of stairs at the back of the house and enter the basement, you are flanked by a pair of stained glass French doors.

It's the door on the right-hand side that leads to an area that members of the crew prefer not to venture on their own.

Over the years, people have sensed a different energy about the space, and there have also been EVPs and photos captured. Small objects were also thrown at an investigator during a solo ghost hunt here.

[NOTE: Due to dark, cramped spaces, set pieces, and tools, this area is off-limits to anyone not on the theatre's crew.]

Hot Spot #4:
The Costume Room Storage Area

There must be something more to the costume room than meets the eye as people have constantly reported activity and uneasiness in there over the years.

If the stairs leading up to the costume room aren't enough to make you turn around and go back downstairs, then perhaps the small storage room just off stage left will.

Today, this room is used for entrances to the upper level of the stage, and many people who have been up there have reported seeing, hearing, and feeling things that they cannot explain.

The uneasiness cast members experience could be because this room is virtually a dead end with the only exit either back through the unnerving costume room or out on stage. Many people claim they feel trapped and refuse to stand up there alone for too long.

Hot Spot #5:

The Spiral Staircase

The spiral staircase is perhaps the most infamous location in the entire theatre. Even audience members seated near the alcove leading to the spiral staircase have reported feeling uneasy or hearing strange noises during a show.

Some believe that the residual energy of a man dwells in and around the staircase. There have been times that people have seen him, heard him, or captured his voice in an EVP on a digital recorder.

The spiral staircase is extremely narrow and steep, causing most to feel claustrophobic. The tight space also makes people feel trapped and panicked, leading some to run out in fear over the years.

A Feeling of Uneasiness

I love the Ghostlight Theatre. I have worked here for over 20 years. It is my sanctuary. When my soul is stormy, I come here for healing. I have sat for hours by myself in the theatre, an audience of one, thinking, figuring things out.

I love it.

Twice over the past 20 years, I have found it necessary to flee the theatre as if my life depended on it.

Both times I was working by myself in the middle of the day, decorating the set—something I love to do. I lock myself in the building and just get to work.

Both times I was hit with a strange and sudden feeling to get out of the building immediately.

Something was coming, and I needed to get out.

I have experienced fierce tornados while I lived in both Missouri and Texas. You hear the siren, and you know you have to seek shelter at once. There is a moment of paralysis followed by a voice in the back of your brain, screaming, "Run!"

That's how I felt here at the theatre on those two occasions. I didn't feel safe until I was in my van with the doors locked, and I was speeding away from the building I love.

What does this mean? I have no idea.

I have never had a panic attack in my life, but I knew my life was in danger.

I like to think I was being warned. But, against what? What happened at the theatre on those two occasions after I left? What was I not permitted to witness?

Maybe it's better I never find out.

-Don Swartz, owner, playwright, director, actor

That damn costume room.

I had to run back and forth through that room many times for both *Nosferatu* (2020) and *Beauty and the Beast* (2019). For some reason (I assume to not interfere with the show), quite often, the lights would be off other than the small light at the end to signal where the door was.

Now I realize that costumes are hanging everywhere with some props here and there, but consistently when I walked past one spot almost directly in the center of the room where there is no vent, it always felt dark and cold.

Please know that when I say "dark" I mean it really felt dark and it looked dark.

For the skeptics out there, it's not that a shadow or an object was interfering with the light source or anything there— it's just a very bizarre area that when you get to it, all of a sudden, you find yourself walking quicker to get to the other side.

I can't tell you that I ever

heard a voice, but I can tell you whenever I arrive at that spot, I feel my hair stand on the back of my neck and immediately walk faster to get to the other end.

-Liz Sanderson, actress

We had just recently acquired the theatre and were still learning the personality of the building. One of the things we found out quickly was that parts of the basement flooded when it rained.

It was spring in 2002 when we were hit with a nasty thunderstorm. A group of us were working on the stage when I decided I should go down to the basement and check the sump pump.

I made my way to the cellar and squeezed myself back into the dark corner where the sump pump is located. After careful inspection, I determined it was running smoothly.

I started heading back upstairs. But after taking a few steps, I quickly realized that someone was behind me.

I say "someone" like it might have been a human being, but I immediately knew it was not. It was large and angry and right up against my back.

I had no intention of turning around.

I was suddenly freezing, and I heard a raspy breathing in my ears.

I took a few tentative steps before breaking out into a full-on sprint. I ran as fast as I could, all the while feeling that presence as if it were attached to me.

Once I got upstairs, I felt free of whatever it was.

I have no idea what it was or why it was angry with me.

I never went into the basement alone after that, and I never told anyone that story. Until just now.

-Jesse Swartz, actor, tech director

On July 30, 2016, I was conducting a ghost hunt at the theatre to reward members who sold $100 in patron ads.

At the last minute, I decided to grab an old object from my office that I had found in the theatre during renovations. It was an old can of Prince Albert Tobacco that had been nestled in a hollow section of a crumbling chimney. The can was empty, but I thought it might help us connect with the spirits.

I asked the participants to sit in a circle on the stage and placed the tin in the middle.

Someone asked what the tin was for, and as I was explaining, I picked up the can and began reading it for the first time.

In big letters on the back of the tin, it said, "Process Patented July 30, 1907."

I didn't know what made me choose that particular relic, but the date proved to be the same as the ghost hunt, only 109 years earlier!

For myself, it was the most productive ghost hunt we ever conducted at the theatre.

-Don Swartz, owner, playwright, director, actor

I have felt unreasonably cold numerous times when using the back stairs by the bathrooms. I have been quite freaked out from that on more than one occasion.

-Barb Fronczak, usher

Anytime I have to go inside the costume room, I keep my head down and move as fast as I can. I always get chills when walking through there. It's not that the room is creepy… I just feel like something is going to pop out and scare the hell out of me.

-Carter Converse, actor

The very first time I visited the Ghostlight was September 2019. I was dropping my son off at the theatre's drama club. It was the first time either of us had ever been there, and I had not yet read or heard about the ghosts.

As soon as we arrived, I felt there was more than living people there.

When we walked in, I was immediately drawn to the staircase to the left of the ticket booth. I felt a strong presence there, and that presence knew I knew  he was there. It is undoubtedly a male spirit, and he definitely did not (and still does not) want me going up those stairs. I didn't feel threatened or that he would want to hurt me or anything, but I felt that he just wanted his space to himself.

I assured him, in my own way, that I would not invade his territory, and he seemed to calm down after that.

Once I walked into the theatre beyond the vestibule, I didn't feel him anymore.

I have felt him every time I have come into the theatre, though, whether it be to drop my son off for drama club or rehearsals, see a show, or usher.

He is not as foreboding as he was that first time, but I still feel like I can't go up in the balcony.

-Tanya Flynt, audience member, usher

December 2000.

We were trying to incorporate in 30 days to take possession of the building that would become our theatre. Our lawyer had the New York State Attorney's Office and me on the phone.

We had to pick a new name for our organization because "Ghostlight Theatre" was already taken by a bookstore in New York City. Our lawyer said if we wanted this to happen by our deadline, we needed a new name on the spot, so I started throwing names out.

One after another—taken.

Desperate, I grabbed a book from my dining room table. I was teaching Art History at Villa Maria College at the time, and I grabbed the class textbook.

I threw the book open and read the first title I came to:

Starry Night Theatre!

I thought for sure that would be taken. But it wasn't! Success!

We had our new name. Now all I had to do was tell our members and our patrons that we had a new name.

I comforted them by telling them that it could be worse: we could be The Raft of the Medusa Theatre.

31

After doing a little research, I began to wonder if anything is truly by chance.

Vincent van Gogh painted *Starry Night* in 1889—the same year our building was being built. He was in an insane asylum in the south of France that used to be a monastery—we create art in a building that used to be a church.

And if you look smack dab in the middle of *Starry Night*, you see our church. Go ahead and get a magnifying glass. It's our building.

It's a perfect name for us.

Luckily, we were allowed to call our building the Ghostlight Theatre.

That's what I have to tell people who are confused when making out a check.

Starry Night Theatre is a group of people.

The Ghostlight Theatre is a building. Buildings can't cash checks!

-Don Swartz, owner, playwright, director, actor

A few years ago, I attended a ghost hunt at the Ghostlight Theatre. I was with my dear friend and the actress who plays Lottie in the *Lottie and Bernice* franchise. Oh, what a fun time we were having! We went up and down and all around!

I have been a season ticket holder for years but only got to see a very limited view of the theatre [until the ghost hunt]. I enjoyed all the back rooms... dark stairwells, seemingly secret places not seen by the average theatre audience!

We made the rounds, and it was our turn to scout out the basement. I had been down there during intermission to grab a candy bar and use the ladies' room many times. It was very different this time... dark and a little disorienting.

We were moving slowly through the hall, going to the restrooms. Out of nowhere, the hair on my arms stood straight up (you don't realize how long your arm hair is until you see it standing up), and it felt as if someone brushed right by me.

At the same time, in my left ear, someone whispered, "She is soooo sick."

I asked out loud, "Who is sick?"

My friend just looked at me. I turned my phone light on to show her the hair on my arms and told her what had happened.

We were both a little shaken.

-Sue Ellen Samuels, audience member

The bell that sits in the bell tower at the theatre was minted in Troy, New York, in 1851. It served as a fire bell for a firehouse in Buffalo when the Friedens Church bought

it and brought it by horse cart to the building on Schenck and Vandervoort Streets.

Some say it is two and a half tons. It has not been rung in a very long time. The last time it was rung, it sent a crack in the wall from the ceiling to the floor in the house right wall. We were told never to ring it.

I often think of the 111 years the bell served to call the faithful to service and to mournfully toll funerals.

If you ever have the privilege to climb the crooked steps up to the bell tower and sit on the top step right next to the bell, you will understand the power the bell still has.

If you dare, reach your hand out and place your open palm on the bell's smooth, flat, cold surface.

It is quiet, but it is far from dead. It vibrates constantly. From the traffic, some say. I don't know. But it does. It vibrates.

It is every bit alive, that I promise you.

-Don Swartz, owner, playwright, director, actor

My one ghost story is very personal and involved a cast member of the theatre who passed away… but there needs to be some background first.

One of the best shows that the theatre puts on is *All Through the Night*. It is a fantastic tale about desperate people spending a Christmas Eve together that would change everyone's lives. I have always loved this show. I saw it the first time in 2006, and it moved me in ways I never knew a show could.

Jed, the young man who passed away, was like family to me, and he loved this show as much as I did.

I considered auditioning for this show in 2009, 2012, and 2015 but could never bring myself to actually audition.

Before the 2018 run, I texted Jed's sister, and asked her if she would be okay if I auditioned. I was hoping to go for the role that Jed had wanted to play before he passed away. It was the same role his sister had played in memory of Jed in the 2015 production.

She told me to go for it, and it was the first show I ended up auditioning for in over 10 years.

I got in, though not in the role I had thought I would get. I was thrilled but nervous.

My ghost story was that Jed was with me that whole run.

During the show, there is a lot of downtime, and when I was on stage, I felt him with me, and I talked to him. My  character had a journal, and I even wrote to him.

I felt like he was there telling me that everything was okay, and that life was going to keep getting better.

Amazingly, it seems so simple… You can just say the words, "He was there," but until you really experience the comfort that someone can give just by letting their spirit come to you, you can't understand the full meaning of those words.

-Sean Polen, actor

When we first moved into the church space, the balcony was primarily taken up by the organ. Our sound and light setups were on folding tables on the side of the

balcony by the spiral staircase (which, to me, is one of the most beautiful areas of the theatre).

There were many times while working sound, I heard steps on the staircase (when the light technician was already in place). There would be breezes up the staircase when the door below was securely shut. Once or twice, I even heard whispers from the staircase.

I never once felt scared of anything in that staircase, or anywhere else in the building frankly. Incidents like these just reminded me we are sharing this space with people who have been here longer than us. I always try to respect that.

-Joy Ann Wrona, actress, usher

Theatre people tend to be superstitious. I am somewhat, but I keep alive a healthy dose of skepticism, especially where mediums, psychics, and others specially connected are concerned.

On a ghost hunt, one woman leaped into the kitchen with unbridled exuberance and proclaimed there were 12 ghosts present! In my mind, I'm thinking, 'Okay, Sparky, settle down,' but, of course, I didn't say that. I just smiled sweetly.

Only one time in 20 years was I impressed by someone's special insight:

The woman was walking across the stage, saying she keeps seeing a coffin.

I told her that there were hundreds of funerals here over the years, and hundreds of coffins laid at the transept before the altar for funeral services.

She insisted that the coffin was lying sideways, extreme stage left.

I told her that made no sense as that's where the pulpit was located. It would not be possible to rest a coffin there.

She kept insisting. In fact, she moved to a spot and said, "Right here!"

And then it dawned on me.

We inherited a real coffin several years earlier when a beloved magic shop on Main Street in Tonawanda closed. We didn't know what to do with a real coffin, so we buried it under the stage.

Guess where?

Right where our psychic was standing.

We pulled the stage apart and had her crawl under it with a flashlight to see it.

She was right.

Only a handful of us knew it was there.

A few years back now, we lent the coffin to a member working on a horror film. We asked him to store it for us, so it is no longer buried under the stage.

My question is: how the heck did she know it was there?

-Don Swartz, owner, playwright, director, actor

I remember one year at the annual membership meeting, we ended the night with a mini ghost hunt. I went up to the bridge [the arch above the stage] with a few people, and the woman leading us stopped dead in her tracks and practically froze in place for a few moments. She said "the cold rushed over her."

I never went up on the bridge ever again... Now whenever I see a show and people are up there, I always think, 'Good thing I'm not in this show! I don't know if I could do it!'

-Erica Schrimmel Bazzell, audience member, actress

There is a spiral staircase in the house right lobby up to the balcony. It spirals up like submarine steps with three lovely stained glass windows to see as you traverse up and down the steps.

It is one of my favorite spots because nobody can see you on either floor if you sit right in the middle of the staircase. I like to hide there and have my coffee before a show or a rehearsal (now the secret is out!).

But if you sit on the bottom step when the theatre is closed, and only a few people are present, you will hear angry footsteps charging down the stairs at you.

I have never met anyone who can stay and see who the footsteps belong to. Like me, they jump up and run out of the lobby as fast as can be. Many people have tried it, all with the same results.

-Don Swartz, owner, playwright, director, actor

A Touching Encounter

While on the annual "cast and crew only" ghost hunt in 2017, I sat up in the attic. It was my first time up in the steeple and anywhere in that area.

I was sitting in a small chair that had been set up for us to use, and while I was holding a mini EVP session, I felt something brush against my hair.

At first, I was afraid I had sat in a spider web and quickly tried to brush it away. When I turned to look, there was nothing near my head.

I tried to ignore it and continued asking questions when I felt it a second time. There was no denying it—it felt like fingers running through my hair!

-Amanda Woomer-Limpert, actress

When I was on a ghost hunt at the theatre, something touched me twice in the costume room—both on my arm and my leg. I still get goosebumps when I think about it!

-Barb Fronczak, usher

I've had something touch my back while in the costume room.

-Carla Kwasniak, actress, crew member

One time I distinctly remember was during *Cabaret* in the summer of 2014. I was on the upper stage left side in the small costume storage room to watch the money scene when I felt a hand brush my neck.

-Courtney Gerou, actress

If you sit on the house right side of the Ghostlight, towards the back and no one is behind you, prepare to feel a tap on your shoulder.

Several patrons have described just such an experience.

One delighted patron greeted me after a matinee and exclaimed that she had met the ghost!

I asked her what she meant, and she described being tapped on the shoulder—no less than three times during the performance, and when she turned around, no one was there!

As she exited the theatre, she turned and with a broad smile, she told me she was going to sit there all the time!

Who is doing the tapping? We don't know. But if you sit there during a performance, you just might have an encounter of the spooky kind!

-Don Swartz, owner, playwright, director, actor

When I first joined the company, I heard the stories of hauntings. Tales of the Lady in Red and other such entities were told as commonly as one would hear about the weather. As someone who loves these stories, I eagerly drank them up every time I heard them, but sadly, the supernatural at the theatre itself initially eluded me.

During the production of *The Innocents* in 2005 (based on the classic novel *The Turn of the Screw*), I got to play Peter Quint, or more specifically, the ghost of said character. I even very briefly got to go on a few dates with the actress who played the ghost of Miss Jessel (I'm not mentioning this to kiss and tell, but it will have relevance).

This is when I started to see things happen. Doors opened of their own accord. We witnessed things actually fall off of shelves backstage. A few people claimed to hear whispers. And then one night, the actress playing the aforementioned other ghost was behind the scenery with me and another actor making some of the spooky special effects happen.

She knelt, facing away from me, probably about five feet away. We heard her whisper, "Stop it."

I looked at the other actor who just shrugged as if to say, 'No idea who

51

she's talking to.' She did this a couple of times, even swatting behind her.

Finally, during a blackout, she hissed through gritted teeth, "Cut it out!"

I snuck up to her and asked, "What are you talking about?"

"We're in the middle of a show," she whispered. "Stop playing with my hair."

I very quickly said that:

A). I get there's a time and place for that and this wasn't it.

B). I was nowhere near close enough to her to have been doing that even if I wanted to.

I later got the other actor to back me up on that as she didn't believe me. I'm still not sure if she does, but she only did the one show with us, and last I heard she moved to Florida (hopefully, not because of me or the handsy ghosts).

-Paul McGinnis, actor

During a performance of *Halloween Dreams* (2011), my mother and sister were sitting in the second to the last row on the right side of the theatre. The row behind them was empty.

During the show, my sister kept feeling a tap on her left shoulder. She even thought it was my mom goofing around. She asked her at intermission, but my mom laughed and said, "I couldn't have reached you if I tried."

My sister seems to attract spirits. So, I am not surprised at all that the theatre ghost tried to communicate with her.

-Joann Mis, actress, music director

I was playing Mina in the 2020 production of *Nosferatu*. Before going out on stage, I prefer waiting in the prop room rather than back in the green room where everyone is talking and hanging out.

Before entering after a particularly sad scene in act two, I was closely watching the monitor, waiting for my cue when I felt someone tug on my dress. Assuming it was the little girl in the production, I turned around to see what she needed… only to find that I was completely alone in the room.

I'm just relieved I managed to make my entrance in time and remember all my lines!

-Amanda Woomer-Limpert, actress

Strange Sights

The Ghostlight Theatre is located on the corner of Vandervoort and Schenck Street in a residential neighborhood in North Tonawanda.

Generally, the neighbors have been receptive and supportive of a community theatre on their block, despite performance dates that find both sides of the streets parked up with our patrons.

So helpful, in fact, are some that I have been stopped on the street several times and told by concerned neighbors that we have left the light on in our bell tower.

One neighbor informed me that the bell tower light's automatic timer must be malfunctioning because they saw the bell tower light flashing on and off. I thanked them for their concern. After all, telling them that they were wrong seemed rude.

You see, the Ghostlight Theatre bell tower rises 80 feet from the sidewalk and offers a great view and always a refreshing breeze.

What the tower does not offer is electricity. The bell tower has no light.

Must have been a ghost light.

-Don Swartz, owner, playwright, director, actor

It was 2001. The show was *Danse Macabre* (the first time we ever saw Lottie and Bernice!).

I was at the theatre with my dad finishing up painting a wall. He went outside, and I was alone in the theatre. I felt something watching me, so I turned to my right and looked over my shoulder.

She was sitting there in the end seat—a woman with dark, curly hair, in a wine-colored Victorian-style dress.

She was gone within a couple of seconds.

I didn't feel anything ominous. She just seemed curious and friendly. I was scared out of my mind, though!

-Justine Swartz, actress, usher

One of the responsibilities of a community theatre's technical director is keeping up-to-date with the latest available technology.

A local radio personality, featured in our 2001 summer musical, had provided equipment to convert our Compact Discs into MiniDiscs.

Late one night in July 2001, a co-worker and I were busy in the sound booth doing just that when she asked who else was in the building. I told her no one. She explained she had just seen a woman carrying something from the hallway behind the stage into the green room. We searched the building, checking the locks as we went, and found no one.

A few months later, my 15-year-old daughter and I were the only ones working in the theatre late one night. I was aiming lights, and she was painting scenery.

I excused myself to step outside for a smoke break. Not two minutes later, my daughter came running out of the theatre, white as a ghost.

She claimed there was a woman in the auditorium watching her paint.

Was it possible that my co-worker and my daughter saw the same woman? I needed to find out.

I called my friend who had helped me convert the discs. I told her my daughter was with me in the theatre, and I intended to ask them questions simultaneously. They agreed. I knew they couldn't hear one another, so I was confident their answers would be their own.

I asked what color the woman's hair was. My friend on the phone answered, "Chestnut," while my daughter pointed to the brunette hair on her own head.

I asked the style of the woman's hair. My friend said, "Piled up in a bun with ringlets around the sides and back." My daughter replied, "Like the wigs the actresses wore in *Little Women*."

What was she wearing? I asked. My friend said, "A floor-length, Victorian-era dress," while my daughter replied, "Like the dresses we wore in *A Christmas Carol*."

Lastly, I asked for the color of the dress. Over the phone, I heard my friend say, "Burgundy," while my daughter replied, "Red."

They had seen the same apparition. I couldn't speak to either of them for a moment. So many thoughts were racing through my head. How many times in life do you get to witness the birth of a legend?

As stunned as I was, two facts were perfectly clear to me:

The Ghostlight Theatre had a resident ghost, and her name was going to be the Lady in Red.

-Jesse Swartz, actor, tech director

On May 2, 2020, there was a live feed investigation where I was alone and walked the camera around so the people watching online could experience first-hand paranormal activity.

This has become my specialty and has become my catchphrase: "First in—Last out."

I was in the basement, exploring the storeroom where the theatre stores props and set pieces for the stage productions. At the one end, the props are placed closely together with a small path that ends at a door with frosted

stained glass that leads back into the art gallery. On the other side of the door was a dimly lit exit sign that cast a light through the door.

I was doing an EVP session, where I asked the spirits of the Ghostlight Theatre to communicate and show themselves.

I was receiving EVP words saying it was trying. That's when I witnessed a figure moving slowly back and forth in the art gallery, blocking out the exit sign light that was filtering through the frosted glass.

I quickly moved into the hallway to see what was causing this anomaly but to no avail. I could not explain it.

After this activity, I moved back into the storage room to continue investigating when I witnessed a small object being thrown. It ricocheted off of something and bounced onto the floor.

I truly believe the entity was playing with me, leading me into areas and trying to scare me out of areas as well.

-Joe Pieri, paranormal investigator

This was over 10 years ago now when we were doing the greatest show that no one ever came to see—*Picnic*!

The set was one of the most ambitious at the time with two two-story functioning houses that we needed to "side" with cardboard.

During winter break, I was off school and decided to help my dad with the siding (it was a goliath task).

At one point, he had to leave to get something from the store. I knew that the building was supposedly haunted, but I also didn't want to look like a scaredy-cat, so I offered to stay at the theatre by myself and continue working. He'd only be gone for about 15 minutes, I tried to remind myself.

While he was out, I played some music to try to keep myself from thinking about the expansive theatre that was right behind my back.

Between songs, I started hearing weird sounds coming from the balcony. A creak here. A knock there.

'It's just an old building,' I assured myself as I continued to work, the hair on the back of my neck standing on end.

Finally, there was a bang so loud that I heard it over the music playing.

I looked over my shoulder to see what it could be and saw a shadow pass in front of the spiral staircase door up in the balcony.

It only appeared for a split second before it vanished. But it was solid and completely blocked out the light shining in through the spiral staircase's windows.

Needless to say, I sighed in relief once my dad came back (the soda and snack he had bought me didn't hurt either).

-Amanda Woomer-Limpert, actress

Back in 2005, during the production of *The Man Who Came to Dinner*, I played the "crazy" Aunt Harriet, who thought she was from the Victorian-era.

I was standing in the kitchen doing prop dishes after my final entrance during a show. I was dressed in a long black dress that looked like it was from the late 1890s.

It felt as if someone was watching me.

I turned around and could swear I saw something, or someone, scurry by the kitchen door. It was like I caught someone watching me.

I wonder now if the spirit thought I was one of the original church members because of my period clothes.

From that show on, I did the dishes the next day when everyone was downstairs before the show!

-Joann Mis, actress, music director

It was during the 2006 one-acts (*The Children's Story*) and I remember being on stage during a rehearsal.

Looking up to the balcony toward the spiral staircase, I saw a woman with dark hair standing there.

I thought it was the director [of the one-act], but then when I looked down, I realized she was sitting in one of the center aisle seats.

When I quickly looked back up at the balcony, whoever it was had vanished.

-Megan Blarr Chapman, actress

We were working in the basement one night, putting set-pieces away and generally straightening up when I saw a little girl in a blue dress and pigtails dash down the long basement hallway and disappear into the theatre's office.

Thinking it was my niece, I followed her and jumped into the office, yelling, "Boo!"

The office was empty.

I asked the other men if they saw a little girl, and they replied that they had seen no one.

Confused, I went upstairs to figure it out.

I stepped into the green room, and there was my niece, sitting in a chair, doing her homework. She wore her trademark pigtails, but instead of a blue dress, she had on black sweatpants and a red shirt.

I asked her if she was in the basement, and she replied that she hadn't been in the basement all night.

I asked throughout the building had any of the other volunteers seen the little girl? No one had.

The thing is: she was a real girl. There was nothing ghostlike about her. She made noise when she ran and had a bright smile on her face. She was real. I know she was.

-Jesse Swartz, actor, tech director

I was in the cast of the 2004 production of *A Christmas Carol*.

During one of the performances, I used the backstage staircase to go down to the basement in between my scenes to use the restroom.

When I got to the basement, through the far doorway of the "Early America" room, I saw a woman in a red dress, walking along the snack bar towards the theatre's office.

I looked down the short hallway along the bathrooms toward the snack bar, expecting to see the woman coming around the corner toward me. But she never appeared.

It was as if she passed by the doorway and vanished into thin air.

I didn't get a sense that I was in danger, but the encounter did take me by surprise.

I decided I could wait to use the bathroom.

-Jennifer McFarland, actress

[NOTE: This encounter occurred before the bathroom remodel. The basement layout has changed since then, and there is no longer a hall from the bathrooms to the office and kitchen.]

This story was told to me by Carl Tamburlin.

During *Joseph and the Amazing Technicolor Dream Coat* (2017)—which was incidentally the last show that Carl would perform in—he would often stick around after we were done with rehearsals so we could walk to our cars together.

As I gathered my things at the edge of the stage, Carl whispered to me, "I saw Jed [Woomer] tonight." [Who died in 2015.]

I looked at him and said, "Where?"

He told me that while he was sitting in one of the center aisle seats during rehearsal when everyone else was on stage, he noticed a shadow by the ghost light.

He said he then saw Jed (wearing jeans and a red T-shirt) peek out from behind the curtain and look at him.

-Joann Mis as told to by Carl Tamburlin, actor

It was after a *Night of the Living Dead* rehearsal (2008), and most of the cast had already left for the night.

I had to run down to the basement to get something, and I noticed the theatre owner's daughter going down the stairs in front of me. I knew it was her because of her long pigtails.

I got what I needed, and then headed back up to the auditorium only to see the owner's daughter sitting with my wife.

It was then that I realized something might be amiss, so I took my wife aside and asked her how long she'd been talking to the little girl. She said about 20 minutes.

It couldn't have been her that I saw down in the basement, nor anyone else because none of the other kids had a similar hairstyle or height. To this day, I still don't know who the little girl was that I saw down in the basement.

-Danny MacKay, actor

In *The Legend of Sleepy Hollow* (2009), the Headless Horseman makes an entrance at the top of the stairs.

During a rehearsal, very early in the party scene, the Headless Horseman appeared at the top of the steps.

I stopped the rehearsal and called out, "You are about 10 minutes early on that entrance, Headless Horseman!"

I was surprised when the actor playing the role called out from the back of the auditorium, "I'm back here!"

Several actors witnessed the figure along with me and all I had to say was, "Go! Go!"

The actors swarmed the backstage area to find the mysterious figure. He was never found.

To this day, we do not know who the shadowy figure was who stepped out on the stage during a fully lit dress rehearsal in full view of a cast of 15 actors.

-Don Swartz, owner, playwright, director, actor

The most unnerving thing that I experienced was going down to the basement restroom during a performance of (what else?!) *Night of the Living Dead*.

No one was down there, and I heard a scratching sound. I turned and looked but didn't see anything.

I walked through what I can only describe as a static electric wall and looked towards the kitchen area. There, I saw a woman smiling at me from behind the counter. I smiled back, looked straight ahead, and looked back at the lady who was no longer there.

I checked the area out and found no one.

-Tim Shaw, audience member

This was during the 2019 production of *A Christmas Carol*.

At one point in the show, the ensemble would sing Christmas songs. My group came from the small area off of the costume room. As we walked onto the upper part of the stage and started singing, I saw a lady in a red dress standing in the center of the balcony directly across from me.

After the song was over, I didn't see her again, and she just disappeared.

I believe in ghosts, but I never experienced paranormal activity until coming to the Ghostlight.

-Stephanie Harper, actress

People who regularly attend Ghostlight Theatre productions know that we call the raised center section in the back of the house the "Peanut Gallery." Many people request the peanut gallery when they reserve tickets. What they may not know is there have been shadowy figures spotted sitting in the peanut gallery when the theatre is closed.

I saw a woman once, sitting quietly.

Other people have reported figures sitting there before they suddenly vanish.

Why they only sit in the peanut gallery, we don't know.

-Don Swartz, owner, playwright, director, actor

I was coming into the theatre one night to pick up my daughter from rehearsal.

I came in and looked up and saw the Lady in Red on the left side of the balcony.

I got scared, so I didn't look up again. I faced the stage, got my daughter, and left.

-Kathy Ellis Donner, usher, actress

One of my first experiences was during *All Through the Night* (2018).

I usually waited by the stairs that lead up to the costume room. I would always stand and wait and watch the monitor. At that time, the director would sit on the stairs with a lantern, editing his new script.

One day while I was watching the monitor and waiting to go on, next to the Christmas tree  where there were no props or actors—clear as day—I saw an adult male leaning against the wall, hands behind his back, with one foot on the ground and the other bent up onto the wall.

It was a shadowy figure, and I believe, based on the shape and lack of hair, that it was Carl Tamburlin.

I even had the director look at it because it was so clear—not a shadow of a doubt that there was someone there.

-Liz Sanderson, actress

I was working sound for *It's a Wonderful Life* (2005) before the booth was built.

I remember pointing out to the light operator how cool it was that they got an actor up on the second story of the house to appear in the window.

He just turned and looked at me before telling me that there's nothing but a wall behind that window—there wasn't enough room for anyone to be standing up there.

I am positive about what I saw, so I must have seen something making an appearance in the window.

-Joann Mis, actress, music director

The very first time I went to the Ghostlight to see my husband in his first show (*It's a Wonderful Life*, 2005), my son and I were walking down the back stairs during intermission.

As we were on the small landing halfway down the stairs, I saw a lady in a burgundy velvet, turn-of-the-century outfit with reddish-brown hair coming up the stairs towards us.

So we wouldn't collide, I stopped and put my arm out to pull my son over a little closer so she could pass.

As I glanced back up at her, she was gone. No one was there.

I was very confused as I knew she didn't have time to run back down the stairs... much less silently. I knew she didn't pass us. Where the heck did she go?

It wasn't scary at all. I just thought it had to be someone from the show in costume.

We went back upstairs after intermission and watched the rest of the performance.

As the show continued, I realized there was never anyone in that type of garb. It was unsettling!

I wondered who she was... Who had that lady been?

Only later did I find out that the theatre was purported to be haunted. Then it all kind of made sense...

-*Carolyn Woomer, actress*

My wife and I were watching *All Through the Night* a few years back. We were in the king and queen chairs in the peanut gallery.

During the scene where the kids were center stage, I saw a kid standing stage left appear to start heading to center stage too early.

I tapped my wife and said, "Well, that kid missed his cue."

She said, "What kid?"

I saw a boy ghost as clear as day that night.

-Greg Hennessy, audience member, actor

Christmas 2015 was painful for many of us.

My little brother, Jed, had just passed away that previous April, and we were performing *All Through the Night*. This is a show that has a special place in every Ghostlighter's heart, and that was true for Jed,  too. He had played both Wally and John over the years, and his goal for 2015 was to be healthy enough to finally play Neil.

I took over his role as "Nell" that year.

It was opening night at the end of curtain call. As we exited down the stage left stairs, my father was the first off, followed by myself.

As I came down the stairs, I saw a tall young man walking towards the ghost light to turn it back on.

In my mind, I thought, 'That's the stage manager.'

As I turned to follow my father into the prop room, the stage manager was there to high five us.

It only took me a second to realize that the young man I had seen wasn't our stage manager... and there was no one else backstage.

A moment longer, and I realized that I knew exactly who I had seen. He was tall and skinny as a beanpole and walked with a very particular gait that I thought I would never see again.

Jed had been with the cast backstage on opening night of *All Through the Night* 2015. And no one can convince me otherwise.

-Amanda Woomer-Limpert, actress

For a project for grad school, I accompanied a team of paranormal investigators overnight at the theatre. I think the group was called the Erie County Paranormal Association.

At some point, a bunch of us just decided to sit in the auditorium and observe in relative silence. I say relative because we were quiet until someone said they thought they saw something moving in the back of the house.

Someone would think they saw something move, and then they would lose the movement.

After a while in the auditorium, I noticed movement too, up in the balcony. It was a shadow, somehow darker than the darkness in the house, pacing back and forth.

The shape in my mind is that of a man, hands behind his back, walking back and forth.

I thought it looked like a choirmaster walking in front of his choir as they sang, listening and taking stock, before giving his singers notes on improvement or words of encouragement.

At the time, I thought, 'Oh, yeah, that makes sense. We are in an old church. There's got to be some residual energy of an old choirmaster up there.'

-Trey Wydysh, actor

86

During musical auditions on several occasions, I would be having casting or production conversations with the musical director.

We would be alone in the theatre waiting for the owner to come up from his office before we closed up for the night.

At least twice, we have both stopped each other mid-sentence and asked, "Did you hear that?"

We would call out, "Is someone there?"

Sometimes, we would hear someone in the balcony.

So, one time after auditions, we decided to ask again if someone was there. When we turned the lights off to leave, we saw what looked like an illuminated shadow of someone—definitely a man—sitting in one of the chairs of the peanut gallery.

We wondered if the lights from the basement were shining upstairs. But, the owner had already come upstairs and turned everything off.

We looked again. Squealing like two scared children— we still saw the illuminated figure.

We shut the door quick, calmed down, and decided to bravely take one more look.

The figure was gone!

Well, of course, that was followed by us screaming, "Oh my God! Oh My God!" and we scrambled out of the theatre!

It doesn't make me a very brave former ghost hunter!

-Joann Mis, actress, music director

I had a very interesting experience once at the theatre after one of our first productions.

There were five of us striking the set in the auditorium.

I was sitting with my back against the proscenium, while the other four men were talking amongst themselves.

I looked up toward the swinging door where the spiral staircase is and saw a misty form in the shape of a woman wearing a long dress cinched at the waist come in through the door. She turned the corner and went down the aisle towards the stairs that lead to the basement.

After she took a few steps, she faded from view.

-Robert Tomasini, actor, crew member

In 2008, I was in a production of *Night of the Living Dead* at the Ghostlight Theatre (I know, I know, very appropriate).

The "zombies" in the show would move throughout the audience, so we had entrances on stage and at the back of the theatre. There was one entrance that was in the small alcove by the spiral staircase. This was my entrance.

It was dark, which I'm sure didn't help my paranoia, but it was also cold—freezing cold. Absurdly cold.

As I waited for my cue during dress rehearsal, I felt a draft hit me. I turned to see if the door was open, but it was locked tight. When I turned back around to face the stage, I saw a shadow on the wall next to my own. It looked human. And then it moved.

I immediately burst from the entrance and declared I wouldn't be using it, so my boyfriend took it instead.

Soon he had a similar experience, and our friend volunteered to take the entrance. He prided himself on being a skeptic.

However, later that night, our director gathered us together and told us that that particular entrance was now off-limits.

I never asked my friend why he gave it up, too. But I don't really think I had to.

-Erin Clare McKay, actress

After my first paranormal experience in 2005, it was as if a door opened, and the ghosts no longer hid from me. In fact, I was to find out that I didn't have to actively look for them at all.

More often than not, I would be in the basement working with a limited crew and see someone walk by me and say hi and wonder why they didn't respond only to confront other people upstairs:

"Hey, who was just downstairs?"

The answers would always be a confused, "No one."

There were also times I would see someone head up to the attic only to find no one there when I went up.

-Paul McGinnis, actor

The tech booth is located in the balcony and housed inside what was once the pipe chamber for the church organ. It is accessed by climbing a few steps and includes counter space for the light board and the soundboard, and two chairs for the operators. Designed specifically for two people, a wooden stool is situated between the boards that is occasionally used for VIPs who wish to view the performance from the best spot in the theatre.

Because the booth is in full view of the actors, the crew is often asked who the third person in the booth is.

I was running lights for a show a few years ago. Sadly, I don't remember which one, but I do remember being asked repeatedly after a Friday night performance who the third person in the booth was.

I told every actor who asked the same thing: we had no visitor in the booth with us.

But they insisted that they saw someone sitting there.

I didn't know what else to say other than I swore to them that there were only the two of us in the booth all night long.

Who several actors saw sitting between us is still a mystery.

-Don Swartz, owner, playwright, director, actor

Did You Hear Something?

While on a small ghost hunt, I was up in the bell tower, sitting directly next to the bell (which in and of itself is incredible).

If you've ever been up there, you'll know that there is a very narrow and very steep staircase that leads to the bell. You're about 80 feet off the ground at that point.

I remember sitting between the bell and the window, just trying to get a feel for the space as I began an EVP session.

After only one question, I heard a loud growl coming from the window to my right.

At first, I thought it was an animal that was on the roof outside the window. But as I looked, I realized that I was even higher up than I originally thought, and there was nothing for an animal to stand on.

To this day, I don't know what growled at me up in the bell tower. I'm curious to see if I ever go back up there if it happens again.

-Amanda Woomer-Limpert, actress

My first experience was in 2001. This one sticks with me well. It was a "clairaudient" [the power to hear something not present to the ear but regarded as having objective reality] experience, making it even more strange.

While waiting to make an entrance as Lottie in *Danse Macabre,* I was in the alcove under the spiral staircase. I was standing in the pitch dark. It was an eerie feeling as we had all talked about the spiral staircase so often.

At the time, the tech crew had their stations for lights and sound right at the top of the stairs. But, that door would be closed during the show making it even darker in that alcove.

I was staring at the window, listening for my cue. This was the Fall show, and the windows had paper decorations on them. One window had a paper pumpkin, and the one I was looking out had a paper skeleton.

All of a sudden, the hair on my neck went up. I heard what sounded like someone coming down the stairs.

I froze, turned, and whispered, "John, is that you?" [The name of the sound tech for the show.]

No answer.

I turned around, frightened, wishing my cue would come quicker.

I started looking out the window again. Very clearly—but clairaudient—in a man's voice, I heard, "That's it… stare at the paper man…"

That sent a chill to my bones. Still does whenever I recall it.

-Joann Mis, actress, music director

Fifteen people of various ages were on a ghost hunt in the theatre in July 2016.

We were seated in the balcony where the church choir used to sing. We decided to sing a verse of "Silent Night" to see if we could stir up anything.

Having directed several musicals, I have concluded that there are four kinds of singers. The non-singer who lip-syncs. The go-along to get-along who sings so quietly that they don't add anything to the overall sound (but they also rarely cause damage). The singer who doesn't know how good he/she is and is always being encouraged to sing out. Finally, the singers who think they are better than they are (you can always pick out these vocalists as they are the ones who sing the loudest).

I had no expectation that the 15 of us would produce anything of a memorable nature.

As we began to sing, I was instantly taken by our beautiful sound.

Being a go-along to get-along singer myself, I felt totally comfortable singing along with these talented singers.

I let my imagination run away with me, and I fancied that I was singing with a large group of experienced singers, and we sounded beautiful.

The verse concluded, and as I looked around, I was met with startled looks on everyone's faces.

A child in the group asked the question we were all pondering: "Who was singing with us?"

Upon discussion, we all experienced the same feeling of being part of a much larger group of singers.

I wish we recorded it.

Sometimes I hear that sound in my head... It was beautiful.

-Don Swartz, owner, playwright, director, actor

Back when we were doing *Oliver!* (2007), I spent much of my time in the prop room. I enjoyed sitting back there because it was quieter than the green room, and I was able to listen to my son, Jed, play Oliver Twist.

During the song "Where Is Love?" I was in the prop room with my daughter listening to Jed sing. I remember being  disappointed one night because the monitor kept getting fuzzy with static right as Jed started to sing! It continued throughout the entire song.

I didn't think anything of it until later when the director and music director came running backstage in a panic.

Apparently, during "Where Is Love?" they kept hearing a voice talking and singing along with the music while sitting up in the balcony.

In hindsight, perhaps the static on the television monitor coincided with the voice they were hearing!

-Carolyn Woomer, actress

I was at the theatre around 11:00pm one night with a few others (the owner's son and daughter) decorating for our friend's birthday. We were the only ones in the building, and everything was locked up.

The three of us were sitting in the green room, chatting, when out of nowhere, we heard clear as day a noise that sounded like someone or something falling down the costume room stairs. It was almost like when you trip walking down the stairs and your feet slide down them while you try not to land on your butt.

All of us jumped up and looked out the door and up the stairs.

We looked, and there was nothing out of place by the stairs, and as I said before, we were the only ones in the building.

-Carla Kwasniak, actress, crew member

One night during a performance of *Yes, Virginia, There is a Santa Claus* (2017), my character, Sister Bernadette, was making one of her many crosses through the costume room to enter on the upper stage left platform.

As I quickly and quietly crossed through the room, I could hear someone moving metal hangers across the metal rods.

I assumed it was the costumer looking for something in the rows of costumes.

I stopped and quietly called to her. She didn't answer. I called a few more times with the same result, but the hangers didn't stop moving across the rods.

I was just about to look down the rows of costumes when an actor in the show popped out from the side room and asked what I was doing.

I told him I thought the costumer was up there looking for something. He said that the other teenage kids in the side room with him were the only ones up there.

Now just to clarify, there are no hangers or metal racks in the side room where the teens were, and the noise was clearly coming from a different area of the costume room.

I didn't tell the teens what was going on, but they ran through that room after our scene very fast...

-Julie Senko, actress, crew member

Back in 2008, we were using the sound booth for video game voice recordings. We had scheduled time slots with a few theatre regulars, and my dad and I were waiting for the next person to show up.

As we were sitting there, we heard the door on stage right open, and then shortly after, the door on stage left.

We both turned our heads in that direction, assuming the next person had arrived and decided to come through that way instead. But no one was there.

About five minutes later, the next person came in talking about how they had just arrived, and they kept apologizing for being late.

-Meagan Swartz, audience member, actress

One of the realities of owning a historic building is relying on the special talents of volunteers.

We had installed a wheelchair lift on the side of the building, and the stairs needed to be reconfigured. One of our volunteers said she would ask the janitor at her church if he would help us out. The janitor said yes. Let us call him Joe.

Joe called me and said the work should only take him a day. He asked if I could come in the morning to let him in and come back at night to see the work and lock up.

I let Joe in one morning and eight hours later, went back to see the work and lock up the building.

When I pulled up to the theatre, Joe was standing out on the sidewalk.

I asked him if he wanted to walk me through the work he did, and Joe said he would never go in our building again. I asked him what happened.

Joe was working and thought he would like some music as he worked. He found a radio on the shelf in the closet and plugged it in and turned it on.

After a while, Joe swore that he heard talking under the music and footsteps in the building. He turned off the radio and listened.

Nothing.

He put the music back on, and the same thing happened again. It was as if the talking and the moving about only happened when the music was playing.

Unnerved, he shut the radio off and went back to work. He went down the hall to use the table saw and suddenly heard music.

The radio had come back on.

He returned to the radio and shut it off again.

Back to the table saw and the music came on again.

That was it.

Joe turned off the radio, unplugged it, wrapped the cord around the radio, put it back on the shelf in the closet, and closed the door.

He was then able to finish the job, and as he started cleaning up, he began to hear a familiar sound. It was far away, but he could tell it was music.

He walked down the long hallway and put his ear to the closet door.

Yes, it was music. The radio was playing. The radio that he had unplugged and put back on the shelf in the closet was playing music.

Joe grabbed his tools and ran out of the theatre.

He said he would never come back into our theatre, and to this day, he hasn't.

-Joe's story as told to Don Swartz

I was running lights for the 2019 production of *The Silver Lady*, a play about a haunted lighthouse.

During intermission, I heard a voice on the intercom, and I figured they were trying to reach us from backstage.

I picked up the walkie talkie and heard whispering and a child giggling.

I told whoever it was to put the stage manager on and stop playing with the intercom system.

The whispering continued.

I handed the walkie talkie to the soundboard operator so she could hear. We agreed that someone in the cast was playing games.

The soundboard operator, wishing to get to the bottom of it, went backstage to see who was playing with the intercom.

The stage manager insisted that no one touched the walkie talkie and, in fact, he had turned it off at the end of act one.

The soundboard operator confirmed it when she returned to the booth: the system was not even turned on.

In that case, who (or what) were we hearing?

-Don Swartz, owner, playwright, director, actor

I was working the house for one of the first spring comedies in the Ghostlight Theatre.

We had invested in headsets so people managing the house could communicate with volunteers downstairs or actors in the green room. It took some adjustment to get used to hearing voices on stage and in my one ear. But doors being rattled, I thought that sound I knew well, regardless of the headset.

I was standing back behind the audience, house right, by the swinging doors that led to the unused entry. And I can swear I heard someone pulling on the outside doors attempting to get in. It sounded to me like the doors could be pulled right off their hinges!

I quickly ducked through the swinging doors, ready to disperse any neighborhood kids on the stoop, messing with the doors. I was shocked that there was no one there.

I quickly wrote off the first time as an adjustment to the headset, but by the third time, I knew it wasn't the headset at all.

I don't know what was trying to get in. But he/she needs to buy a ticket first!

-Joy Ann Wrona, actress, usher

112

It was after crew one day when everyone had gone home. Someone forgot to close the doors, so I said I would run in and do it.

After I shut the green room door, I turned to close the door leading into the theatre. All of a sudden, I heard three or four different kids laughing. It kept getting louder and sounded like more kids.

I was so freaked out—I ran down the stairs and out the door!

-Justine Clark Fritz, actress

When I was a teenager, I had to pass through the basement to enter at the back of the house for *Night of the Living Dead* (2007).

The lights wouldn't turn on, so I was walking through the dark and heard someone whisper in the kitchen area.

I couldn't quite make it out, but it sounded like half of a conversation.

I was only 15 or 16 years old, so I ran right out of there!

-Courtney Gerou, actress

I stage managed the production of *Deep End of the Dark* (2013).

One of the stage manager's main duties is to set the stage and props before each performance. I would  normally get there early and start straightening and setting the props.

When I entered the theatre there was a lot of noises coming from the house. I only had on the work lights and ghost light. I didn't want to go through the house and up to the booth to get the house lights.

I normally try to talk to the noises. Why?

1. Hoping they'd stop.

2. To ease my mind.

This time it didn't work. So I went outside until some of the cast and crew showed up.

-Julie Senko, actress, crew member

There are two ways you can get tickets by phone at the Ghostlight Theatre: I answer the phone and take your order, or you leave your order on the machine. That's it. No one else answers the phone. The phone is in my locked office, and I am the only one with a key.

So it was strange one summer when two ladies on two separate occasions told me they tried to place a ticket order, but the person who answered the phone just breathed heavily on the line, laughed, and then abruptly hung up. Both called back and got the same response.

I explained to them that my phone persona is flat and grumpy, but I would never breathe heavily, laugh, and hang up.

They both insisted they dialed the right number.

I didn't know how to respond... Someone or something had answered the phone in my locked office!

-Don Swartz, owner, playwright, director, actor

Back in 2002, I spent my days that summer painting the walls and ceiling inside the theatre. I would arrive every day, gather my supplies in a bucket, and turn on the radio. I would then make the arduous climb up the professional painter's scaffold we borrowed (it was much bigger than the one we have at the theatre now, so getting up and down was a little bit of a scary pain) and I would position myself and pull up my bucket of supplies.

Every time I would get to the top, I would hear what sounded like someone coming in the side door or around the corner from the hallway as if to enter the theatre.

I would turn my radio down, say, "Hello?" to an empty room, and hear no reply.

I climbed down several times and found no one in the building. I finally said out loud to who or what might be listening, "I am here to paint and make everything look nice. So, please don't try to talk to me now."

I really think it was the spirits trying to talk to me.

-Joann Mis, actress, music director

The last three times that *All Through the Night* has been performed on the Ghostlight stage, I've had the privilege to run sound.

During the 2018 production, it was not uncommon for me to arrive early on performance nights to check all my sound cues, usually before the cast and crew showed up.

The booth is located in the theatre's balcony. Next to the entrance of the booth is a flight of stairs leading up to the attic and bell tower. In this area, people have experienced strange sounds and shadows. There are only two ways up to the balcony—both are easily viewed from the booth, so you'd know if anyone was up there with you.

Several times, I've felt uneasy in the theatre when I was alone... especially in the balcony.

One particular evening, I was in the sound booth, and I knew that the director and I were the only ones in the building so far, and he was in his office in the basement.

As I was checking my sound cues, I heard a voice from behind me whisper my name. "Gary..."

I paused what I was doing and looked around, thinking I had imagined it.

The booth is very narrow, and there's only room for about three or four people. I was alone.

I went back to what I was doing, and there it was again: "Gary…"

It seemed to be a woman's voice.

I got up and looked around the balcony, and there was no one there. Once again, I went back to my soundboard, and I heard the voice a third time.

I went downstairs and waited for someone else to show up before I headed back to the booth.

It only happened that one time during the run, and I have worked in the sound booth many times over the last 10 years—I haven't experienced it before or since.

I still go up to the booth alone… but it's not one of my favorite things to do.

-Gary Cox, actor, crew member

We decided to hold a small ghost hunt after a rehearsal in 2018, so it was pretty late at night.

I had to use the bathroom, so I headed downstairs. There's a short hallway leading to the restrooms, and when I was walking back to the stairs, I heard a deep voice behind me say, "Hello."

I turned around, but there was no one there.

I was pretty freaked out, so I just booked it to the stairs and got away from there.

-Carter Converse, actor

In October 2015, during a rehearsal for *Murder in the Smoky Mountains*, one of the actresses sitting in the auditorium stopped rehearsal and asked everyone what that noise was.

We all got quiet, and we quickly became aware of a pounding noise coming from the balcony. It was like the sound of two pieces of wood being slammed together. The only problem was: no one was in the balcony.

I went upstairs to investigate.

As I got to the top of the steps, the noise suddenly stopped.

I looked around.

Nothing.

After a while of searching, I got an idea. I asked the cast to listen to the sound I was about to make and see if it was the same as they heard. I made the noise, and instantly everyone agreed that was the noise we all heard over and over during rehearsal. They asked how I made it.

We had old wooden seats in the balcony—the kind where the seat is on a spring and only goes down when someone sits on it.

I pushed the seat down and then quickly pushed it upright, creating a slamming sound. We had heard it about a dozen times in a row.

Who or what would do that in the middle of a rehearsal with so many witnesses? We still don't know.

-Don Swartz, owner, playwright, director, owner

I was part of a ghost hunt at the Ghostlight in 2016. Small groups of us investigated various parts of the theatre on a rotational basis so we could be secluded, have some quiet time, and not have any noise pollution from other groups.

In complete darkness, I sat by myself halfway up the spiral staircase. I sat there, asking some questions, hoping to get a response. I did not hear a voice. What I heard was much more unsettling.

I heard footsteps coming down the stairs right behind me. You could even hear the crunching of shoes on debris on the stairs as someone—or something—stepped closer and closer to me.

I came flying out of that stairwell, screaming and cursing my fool head off. I think I looked like a cartoon character with my eyes bugging out of my head. It was absolutely terrifying!

-Carolyn Woomer, actress

Over the years, when we would have sleepovers at the theatre, I would hear A LOT of people walking around in the attic above where we slept.

-Carla Kwasniak, actress, crew member

I started to volunteer to "theatre sit" when ghost hunters would come for overnights because:

A). I was fascinated by them.

B). I didn't sleep much, so I was the best guy for the job.

As a whole, I tried to stay out of the way of the ghost hunters that came through the theatre, knowing they were just there to investigate, and any "help" could skew what they were attempting.

I remember one such group who seemed put out by my presence, keeping me out of their opening prayers that were basically asking the ghosts not to hurt them. I joked after that I'd prefer they don't hurt me either. This further annoyed them.

I told them that I'd stay out of their way and only asked they don't go into the attic alone because parts of the floor were easy to fall through, and I didn't want anyone injured.

Halfway through their hunt, one ran downstairs, yelling he was up in the bell tower (a part of the attic he wasn't supposed to be in) and that a voice told him it was "not of God" but of something else.

I highly doubted there was anything malevolent in that place and that if you came into my space without permission, I'd probably yell evil things at you as well, but kept that to myself.

Still, I took that moment to reiterate the dangers of going into places without the proper guidance for safety purposes. This served to annoy them more, and they left me out of the closing prayer too (don't follow us home or hurt us, ghosts... but do whatever to that guy was how I read it).

At the end of the night, I told them it was best we all leave together—it was 4:00am at that point, and the neighborhood wasn't necessarily the best at the time. I asked them to give me a minute to shut down the lights, and I'll walk them out. Just because they didn't want me protected from the ghosts didn't mean I wanted them hurt by the living.

I checked the attic door, and as I did, I felt a cold breeze, which told me they went all the way up the tower into the belfry, which was very much off-limits for safety reasons. That and the fact that sometimes bats lived up there was another reason we shouldn't leave that door open. Which they did.

So, up the stairs I crept in the pitch black while talking to whatever was up there:

"It's just me! No worries! You know me! Sorry to get into your space... I'm just going to shut this door."

I began pulling it into place, and I felt it push shut from the other side. Sure, it could have been the wind.

Could have...

But I'm not sure I hit every step as I scrambled back down the stairs.

"Okay, I'm ready!" I called to the rest of the team, only to be met with silence.

I searched the theatre only to find it empty. Not only that, but they also left the back door completely open so anyone could have just wandered in (I did explicitly tell them it wasn't the best of neighborhoods at night, didn't I?).

Once again, proving it's not the dead we have to worry about sometimes.

-Paul McGinnis, actor

127

I spend a lot of evenings alone in my office in the basement. Some nights, I hear nothing. Some nights, I hear a crowd of people in the auditorium on the first floor. It sounds like a lot of people walking around, slamming doors, and moving things. Sometimes it seems like soft mumbling from miles away.

I never go check. I don't want to know.

One night, I called out for them to quiet down up there. They did.

But that was not all: I could not hear anything. Nothing! For a few seconds, I was stone deaf. I could hear nothing. As if my head was packed with cotton.

I finally reached out and grabbed a pencil and started tapping on my desk. Eventually, I heard the tapping, and my hearing came back. But the first three or four taps, I could not hear.

It was truly terrifying. I never told the spirits to quiet down after that.

-Don Swartz, owner, playwright, director, actor

One night, during dress rehearsal for *A Christmas Carol* (2019), I was walking down the tiny, dark hallway going into the green room. It's only lit by one lamp, but the lamp happened to be off that night.

As I was walking, since it's such an old building, I could hear the floor creak under my feet. Right after my foot would make a creak on a floorboard, I'd hear the same creak again from the floorboard behind me.

I assumed it was one of my co-stars following me into the green room, but when I turned around to say hello, no one was there.

-Ariana Rose, actress

The spiral staircase is one of my favorite places in the entire theatre. While some people refuse to go in there, I love sitting in the middle of it where you can't see the top or the bottom.

I was on a ghost hunt and found myself sitting alone in the spiral staircase. While sitting there, I heard a man's voice murmuring.

At first, I thought someone was out in the theatre or on the stage talking (sound does travel into the staircase fairly easily). I looked out into the theatre to find only the two women in my group sitting in silence, so I went back to sit in the staircase.

Sure enough, the man began talking again.

It almost seemed as if he was oblivious to me, or possibly stuck in a loop, talking to himself. Either way, there was no man out in the theatre whose voice would have traveled into the staircase like that.

Combine that with another experience I had in there with a man saying my name, and you've got a chatty ghost hiding out in the spiral staircase!

-Amanda Woomer-Limpert, actress

While we were doing the musical *Beauty and the Beast* (2019), Gaston, LeFou, and I were in the basement just talking and sitting in the area with all the picture frames of the past shows [the "Early America" room].

There was an old radio that's been used as a prop many times. It was never plugged in, and we didn't go anywhere near it, but it turned itself on and started playing the sinister music programmed into it.

Not once, not twice, but three times this happened while we were talking.

Gaston was pretty freaked out by the third time and rushed back upstairs with LeFou right on his heels.

-Nathan Schuh, actor

During *A Christmas Carol* (2019), I was ready a little earlier than the other cast members in a scene, so I went upstairs to my spot in the costume room storage area.

It was pitch black when I was in the costume room as I made my way to the small storage area (upper stage left). Usually, the costume room light is on too, but for some reason, it wasn't this time.

Once I stood in my place, I heard this old man's voice telling me to "Go away!"

Twice, he said it in an angry tone like he didn't want me there.

The room was already cold when I got there, but I felt like he was directly in front of me right at the curtain. But I saw nothing, and when I reached my hand out in front of me, I felt nothing either.

Once the other cast members were upstairs with me, I didn't hear anything again.

-Stephanie Harper, actress

During a Saturday morning crew session, a member of the costume crew went up to the second floor's costume room to pull some pieces.

As she was up there, she heard laughter and saw someone running through the costume racks.

"Good one, guys. You got me!" she said to the four children she was sure were pranking her. "I'm going back downstairs. You are going to be up here all alone. Serves you right!"

She left the costume room, laughing and shaking her head.

She came down the steps to the green room and was shocked to see the kids playing there.

She asked them if they had pranked her in the costume room, and they promised her they never left the green room.

A group of us went upstairs and searched the costume room. We found nothing.

"I heard them! I saw them!" was all she could keep saying.

We believed her.

-Don Swartz, owner, playwright, director, actor

I used to hear a lot of noises coming from the costume room when I played Past in *A Christmas Carol* (2019). I would be so scared when I had to exit.

I would enter the little room with all the fabric and just close my eyes and wait for someone to get me for two reasons:

1. I couldn't walk in my costume.

2. I was scared I would see the ghost that was making all the noise.

It was like that every night.

-*Carla Kwasniak, actress, crew member*

I was at crew, working on the set for *The Haunting of Hill House* (2020). I was paired with a fellow crew member, and we were taking down a screen from the stage. I was holding it, and she was using a drill to take out some of the screws.

While we were working, she told me about one of the ghosts of the theatre—one that has been captured in a photo of a pair of doors (page 180).

Suddenly, there was a loud bang that shook the entire stage. I thought my fellow crew member had dropped the drill, but I looked, and she still had it in her hand. She immediately reacted as well and asked if I felt/heard that.

I replied, "Um… Yes!" How could I not?

She felt a pound under her feet along with the loud bang. Everyone at crew heard it.

On top of all this, the doors that she had been telling me about were right behind us on stage.

-Vanessa Stipkovits, actress, crew member

Long before the sound booth was built out of the old church organ, the balcony looked very different! The light board and soundboard operators sat up in the balcony, out in the open.

I had only recently joined the Ghostlight family and was eager to learn how to run lights (which, ironically, I still haven't done even 15 years later).

During the final dress rehearsal for *Here We Sit* in May of 2006, I sat up in the balcony with my dad, who was running lights. We were on the house right side of the balcony along with the soundboard operator.

During one of the scenes performed by nothing more than a collection of stuffed  animals to an epic soundtrack, I heard a man laugh in my ear.

When I turned around to see who it was, there was no one there... but it came from the direction of the spiral staircase.

I've heard the man's laugh several times over the years since then, most recently at a performance of *The Lottie and Bernice Show* in May 2019. I only hear it in the balcony when no one else in the theatre is laughing.

-Amanda Woomer-Limpert, actress

On August 8, 2008, the Ghostlight hosted the first of three paranormal investigations for Soul Seekers United.

With the investigation beginning shortly after 11:15pm, the team split up to perform temperature and EMF baseline readings of the entire building. While wandering through the art gallery, the team distinctly heard a whistle coming from the kitchen area on two separate occasions.

This is important to note because, in theatre superstition, it is bad luck to whistle inside a theatre. To outsiders, this may seem like a bizarre rule that actors follow, but we take it very seriously at the Ghostlight Theatre.

Why? Well, back in the day, stagehands would use whistles as cues to know when to raise and lower backdrops. Sandbags acted as counterweights for the backdrops, sometimes resulting in tragedy if they raised or lowered the backdrop at an inopportune moment.

Nowadays, many actors believe if you whistle inside a theatre, you risk something falling on you.

After getting some inconsistent EMF readings (a spike jumping from .02 to 24.0), they decided to conduct an EVP session in the green room. Multiple people reported hearing heavy breathing, humming, singing, and even music throughout the EVP session... Where was this music coming from? They never did find out.

-Taken from the case files of Scott Schultz and Soul Seekers United

It was read through for *Twisted Tales from the Golden Days of Radio* (January 2020).

The full cast and crew assembled around a table on the stage, waiting for two actors. These same two actors are notoriously late for rehearsals. We will call them Mr. F and Mr. W.

As the cast was waiting for them to arrive, we started making bets on who would walk through the door first. We even stipulated that Mr. F represented the San Francisco 49ers, and Mr. W represented the Kansas City Chiefs, and whoever entered first would predict who would win the Super Bowl.

Finally, we heard the door to the outside open and slam. We heard footsteps on the stairs. We heard the door to the auditorium open. We waited, all anxious to see who would walk through the curtains. And it was… no one.

There was no one there.

But we heard it…

People come and go at the theatre all the time, and sometimes you can't see them.

Mr. F and Mr. W did eventually arrive, and yes, Mr. W entered first and assured us all that the Kansas City Chiefs would indeed win the Super Bowl.

Just another night at the Ghostlight!

-Don Swartz, owner, playwright, director, actor

My dad and I were auditioning for a play (unfortunately, I can't remember which one), and we were the last people there.

I sat downstairs on a bench by the bathrooms and waited for my dad to finish his audition (it was a monologue audition instead of a cold reading) when I suddenly heard the water running in the women's bathroom. It didn't last long. It just sounded like someone was washing their hands. But no one came out, and I started to think that I imagined it.

Then, sitting there, I felt my hair moving on the right side of my head, as though someone was playing with it.

I freaked out and ran upstairs and got my dad (who had luckily finished auditioning), and we left.

-Megan Blarr Chapman, actress

I attended a ghost hunt in 2006-2007 with a local paranormal group.

I was gathering EVPs over by the stage when I asked if the ghost spoke German. When listening back on my digital voice recorder, I could clearly hear the word "Geist" exclaimed under my talking [German for "ghost"].

-Joann Mis, actress, music director

Lots of different things happened to me during *Cabaret* (2014).

At one point, I would enter on the upper stage left platform, so I had to wait in the costume storage room for a while during every performance.

One night, I heard a young woman giggle after some costumes moved on the hangers.

Another night, there were many more footsteps than there were people up there.

-Courtney Gerou, actress

It was February 2001.

We had acquired the building that would become the Ghostlight Theatre a month prior.

I was sitting in my cold basement office when I started to doze off.

I immediately heard a small group of women shouting, "Don't ever fall asleep in this building!"

I woke with a start. What the heck was that? I heard it loud and clear but in my head. It was urgent and sincere. I took it as a warning.

I only violated the rule once, and I will never forget it.

I fell asleep in the office a few years later. The moment I was fully asleep, I was greeted by the people and events of this building from the last century, all at once.

A mass of people, and yes, things and events came hurtling at me like a freight train—all wanting attention at the same time.

I woke with a scream, and I finally understood what the warning meant:

It wasn't to keep me from being afraid—because I was anyway. It was to keep me sane.

I think if all of a century descended on me at one time and desired to be processed all at once, I would probably short circuit and go... well, to use Poe's words: stark raving mad.

There have been sleepovers here at the theatre for the young people, but I have never attended, and I never will.

Nobody else has experienced this, and I am happy for them.

-Don Swartz, owner, playwright, director, actor

A Moving Performance

A couple of years ago, Carl Tamburlin and I were cleaning up the concession area after intermission.

My Stephen and Carl were always teasing one another (Stephen at this point had died back in 1999). We were joking that if Stephen were here, he'd have a comment to make.

Suddenly, a picture that had been secured on the ledge flung onto the floor.

Carl and I just looked at each other and felt it was Stephen's way of letting us know he was with us.

-Joan Kantor Holesko, box office manager

Performing in *Arsenic and Old Lace* (2002) was a huge deal for me. I was so very proud to be playing one of

the sisters, Abby, and being with such an amazing cast that was working extremely hard and playing just as hard.

I was usually the first to arrive for rehearsal and entered the building with the director. And more often than not, we were the last two to leave the building as well.

We kept noticing things changing on the set when we arrived. We thought maybe cast members were pranking each other, as had become the thing to do.

So one night, when we left, we intentionally reviewed the entire set and marked where everything was, including all the artistic busts on the set. I remember distinctly him saying to me, "That one, right in the center is facing stage left. Do you see it?"

When we arrived the next day for rehearsal, we went straight to the theatre. And it was facing stage right.

We were the last ones out and the first ones in. Apparently, the prankster has not left the building for a long time.

-Joy Ann Wrona, actress, usher

My office is in the basement, sandwiched between the restrooms and the snack bar. Not too bad, really! The drinking fountain is right outside my door, so I really do have everything I need right there.

One night, I was at the theatre alone, in my office, and I heard the sink come on in the men's room.

I walked in and turned the water off and went back to my desk.

A few minutes later, the water came on again, full blast, in the sink—both cold and hot.

I turned it off and went back to my office.

Another night, I was alone in the theatre, in my office, and I heard the fan go on in the ladies' restroom. There are four automatic stalls, and the light and fan go on when someone enters the stall.

I went to look.

The door was closed, but I could see the light was on and I could hear the fan running.

I waited.

The fan turned off, and the lights went off.

I knocked.

Nothing.

Slowly, I opened the door. No one was inside.

What do these occurrences signify? I have no idea. That is the nature of a true haunting: most of the time, they make no sense whatsoever!

-Don Swartz, owner, playwright, director, actor

The only thing that ever happened to me was when I went to see *Yes, Virginia, There is a Santa Claus* (2017).

Unfortunately, the guy I went with was someone I had just broken up with at the time (awkward, I know), but we still went together to see the show.

I was in the first row of the peanut gallery right at the end where the pillar is. I didn't want to sit near my ex, so I leaned on the pillar during the majority of the show.

Then at one point, it felt like the entire pillar moved, and I even fell over a tad.

So then it was really awkward for the rest of the show because I was afraid to lean on the post but didn't want to sit anywhere near my ex!

I don't know if it was a ghost, but it was definitely eerie! It felt like a spirit knew I was trying to get away from him and wanted to prevent me from doing so.

-Jill Anderson, actress

While in *It's A Wonderful Life* (2008), there was a scene where we all had fake candles. I always hid mine on top of a shelf in the green room's back corner because I was paranoid that someone would take it. There were only so many to go around, and no one but me knew it was there.

On one of the off nights, there was a paranormal hunt of some sort. The theatre's owner said when they went into the green room, one of the lights was randomly on. He showed me a picture, and it was the one I kept hidden!

So not only was my secret hiding place exposed, but I also had a haunted candle.

Usually, I'd be a skeptic and think that somebody turned it on for pure shock value, but the fact that no one knew I had been keeping it there definitely makes me think something unexplainable happened to turn it on.

-Gabe Neumann, actor

155

We were in the middle of rehearsals for *The Music Man* (2016). The barbershop quartet was practicing our songs for the show in the green room—it was just the four of us.

If anyone knows about the green room doors, they know that these doors don't easily open when they're completely closed. They also tend to swing open if not secured. However, the four of us know that the door was tightly shut on the stage right side of the green room so we wouldn't be interrupted.

Well, it seems our ghost had other plans or was being a critic.

We were standing in the middle of the green room when the door slowly opened by itself while we were singing. We all just stopped and looked at each other.

We closed the door and continued our rehearsal. The door swung open again.

This time, we ran over to see if someone was on the other side. There was no one. There was no time to run up the stairs to the costume room, downstairs to the basement, or back into the auditorium. Not to mention if someone had opened the door and run away, we would have heard footsteps on the stairs or the door to the auditorium close.

So, to this day, we are all convinced it was the theatre's ghost.

-Gary Cox, actor, crew member

Once I was staying late working on the lights and set with the tech crew.

As we left, I saw them shut everything off and lock up.

The next morning, I returned with them when we found the wallpaper on the set had been trashed overnight, ripped off when nobody had been in the building.

We had forgotten to turn on the ghost light. Apparently, the spirits went all ham on the set as a result!

-Steph Wiechec Luss, actress

The first Christmas show after Jed Woomer passed away (2015), we were sitting backstage before the show.

The kids started talking about Jed and how if he were still here, he would be on stage with them or at least hanging out in the green room with them.

At that point, the green room door opened, and no one was there... Well... that's not what we think...

-Julie Senko, actress, crew member

On October 17, 2008, the Ghostlight Theatre hosted the second of three paranormal investigations for Soul Seekers United.

While none of the investigators walked away with personal experiences on this particular investigation, they were given a bit of a show from our very own ghost light.

Shortly into their German language EVP session, the ghost light would continuously turn on. Then, after approximately 15 minutes of illuminating the house, it would turn off once more.

At one point in the evening, a female investigator asked the light to turn on for them. It did. To test the light once more, she then asked it to turn off. It promptly obeyed once again.

Within less than a minute, she had the light turning on and off, not once, but twice.

No one else on the team was able to command the light as she did.

-Taken from the case files of Scott Schultz and Soul Seekers United

I have been a part of the Ghostlight Theatre on and off for almost 15 years, and I can say that I genuinely believe that it is haunted... though I am not overly fond of the connotation that the word gives. Many people think of "haunted" as a negative thing, but the spirits I have felt at the Ghostlight have either been comforting or playful.

An example of the latter was during the auditions for one of the musicals. I have played for these auditions on several occasions, but this specific time was after an absence of some years.

The ceiling at this point definitely needed a "pick me up," and those of us in the room were making comments to that effect.

The music director commented that Carl, a beloved theatre member who had recently passed away, would be lecturing her on how much the paint job needed a touch-up. No sooner had the words left her mouth, than a large paint chip fell down right next to her.

We all took it as a good laugh as Carl had always been a great prankster in life, and would have found it hysterically funny to scare us right at that moment.

No other paint chips have fallen before or since that day, and I take it as a parting message from our dear friend.

-Sean Polen, actor

For the production of *Angels in Love* in the spring of 2003, we placed two romantic statues—one a boy and one a girl—on opposite sides of the stage facing each other.

Every night we'd come in for rehearsals, and the statues would be turned away from each other.

This happened every night, even through the performances. We could never figure out who was turning the statues to face away from each other.

I have a theory:

The Ghostlight Theatre was a church for 111 years before it became a theatre. *Angels in Love* is the story of a  randy teenaged Little Lord Fauntleroy on the prowl for romantic conquests. It's very funny, but a little naughty.

I got to thinking that maybe one of the spirits was not pleased we chose to tell this story in their church!

-Don Swartz, owner, playwright, director, actor

During *A Christmas Carol* (2019), I helped tidy up the green room before the show started, and I put a skeleton from the fall show in a black body bag to be taken up to the costume room. The bag was completely zipped up in the corner by the armoire.

So the next rehearsal, the head costumer came up to me asking about the skeleton because it scared her. She asked if I left the bag unzipped on purpose.

I told her I definitely did not leave it unzipped because:

1. That's creepy.
2. It would have scared me!

So I went up with her and low and behold, the bag was unzipped halfway with the skeleton sitting upright.

We had a good laugh over it and left it to creep on the rest of the cast for the remainder of the show.

I'm not 100% sure if this was paranormal or someone playing a prank on us. But that corner definitely has a foreboding feeling to it that I have felt before, and once I leave that corner, I don't feel it anymore. The rest of the building has a real calming feel to me, so I hope the rest of the spirits there are happy that we are here.

-Allie Schnackel, actress

During *Marvin's Room* (February 2007), I was in the kitchen on the phone, sitting at the table facing the door. While talking, I noticed one of the flyers pinned to the wall near the kitchen door waving in the breeze.

After a minute or two, it dawned on me that we were inside, so I looked for a vent or fan and couldn't find any source of where the draft was coming from.

I quickly ended the call and hauled it upstairs, too freaked out to be down there.

-Tommy Vane, actor

The very first experience I ever had at the Ghostlight was during crew for the 2006 one-acts: *The Children's Story* and *A Rose for Emily*.

I was working in the green room (back when it was still green!) with two members of the costume crew when we heard someone running around above us in the costume room.

The two ladies went upstairs to tell the kids that they shouldn't be running around up there, and me being the new kid, followed behind.

When we got up there, the door to the costume room was closed and the lights were off. As we opened it, we saw a cluster of hangers rocking back and forth on a nearby rack as though someone had just run past it to hide.

Needless to say, the kids were not up there—no one was—and we quickly ran back down to the green room!

-Amanda Woomer-Limpert, actress

The only experience I really had was when I was working sound for *Arsenic and Old Lace* (2002), and someone—or something—pushed my headset on my head.

It had been falling back and I was thinking I had to push it back up. But before I could reach up and do it, the headset moved on its own.

I didn't feel scared or anything… it just happened.

-Mallory Allen, actress

During a particular scene in *The Silver Lady* (2019), everyone else was on the main stage, describing how they thought the murders happened. My character, Miranda, was in the attic doing her psychic investigation.

I would light candles, smudge the space with both sage and Palo Santo. I would then use the pendulum.

I never did anything to manipulate its movements, but every time I got to this point, the pendulum would always spin on its own. Some days it was much more active than others, but the swing of it would usually point house left

towards the balcony. I have some psychic abilities in real life and have always sensed a presence in that area.

Next, I would get out the divining rods. I would hold them out in front of me and quietly ask that they be moved in one direction or another. I have no idea how one would even manipulate divining rods to make them work that way.

This I would come to truly believe was Carl Tamburlin, and once I began to ask him by name to move the rods, their movement was more precise and would always move how I asked.

"Carl, move them away from each other. Move them left. Point them towards each other."

And he always did exactly as I asked.

-Sara Jo, actress

Caught on Camera

One in a series of photos taken by Sarah Fronczak Taravella on the night of the 2016 ghost hunt.

The left-hand side is the original photo, and the right-hand side is the encircled area.

"The scariest part of it was I took those photos and didn't look at them right away, so I didn't see the face.

"We all went on stage and turned off the lights and just sat. My cousin's (ex) boyfriend and I both saw a shadow walk real quick in that corner [leading to the spiral staircase].

"I literally get chills thinking about it."

The photo on the left was taken on Joann Mis's cell phone during the 2017 ghost hunt in the storage area next to the stairs in the basement. The photo on the right is a family photo from the Woomers of their son, Jed, when he was about 11 years old.

Jed passed away in 2015 at 19 years old, but not before having been an active member at the theatre—most memorably portraying Oliver Twist in the 2007 production of *Oliver!*

The similarities between the photo of young Jed and the ghostly photo in the basement are uncanny—you can see his long brown hair, jawline, T-shirt, and some even claim to see his backpack.

Joann did not have access to the family photo before or on the night of the ghost hunt when she captured this photo on her phone.

To add to this evidence of Jed's spirit at the Ghostlight, at the same ghost hunt, his big sister, Amanda, was conducting an EVP session in the basement. As she made her way over to the storage area next to the stairs, she asked Jed, "Dude, are you okay? Just let me know that you're okay."

In the same place this photo was taken, she captured an EVP of his voice (from when he was about 11 years old), assuring her and everyone else at the Ghostlight, "I'm fine!"

Orbs are a popular topic of debate in the paranormal. To some investigators, they are the manifestation of a soul or spirit—a sphere is far easier for a spirit to show itself rather than a full-bodied apparition. For other investigators, orbs are nothing more than dust, bugs, condensation, etc.

This photo, taken by Scott Schultz and his team during their 2008 investigations, is interesting because of its location:

Many people have reported seeing ghostly figures sitting in the peanut gallery over the years.

Could this orb be a spirit sitting in their favorite chair, waiting for a show to start? There's no true way to know. However, we can't forget the number of times we've seen or heard some unusual things in our beloved peanut gallery.

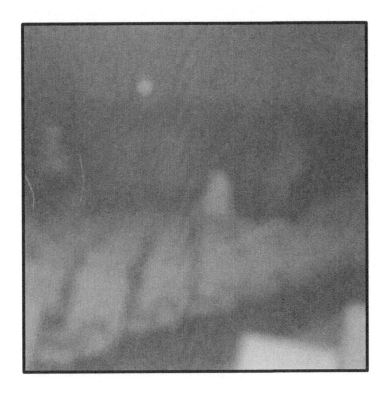

This photo was taken by music director, actress, and former ghost hunter, Joann Mis at the 2017 cast and crew ghost hunt.

Many believe it shows a spirit siting in the back row of the auditorium where people have reported being touched in the past.

Many believe this photo captures the face of a man in the French doors stored down in the basement. It was taken by Scott Schultz and his team on a paranormal investigation on December 12, 2008.

According to Schultz:

"While in the basement, I thought I heard some noise out in the hallway. Sitting in front of the [camera] monitors, I just raised the camera and took a picture out into the hall.

"I was looking at the picture and lightened it up and saw what looks to be a face in the door window…

"To me, it almost looks like he seems to be wearing Shakespearean clothing [an Elizabethan ruff] and has a mustache."

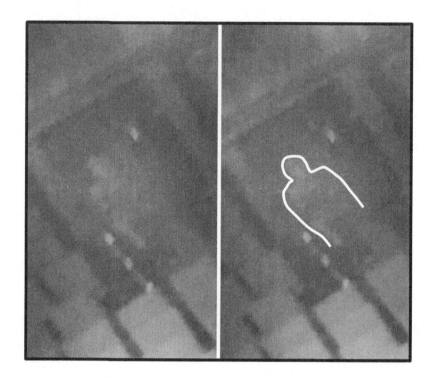

Rachael Martinez took this photo on the night of the July 2016 ghost hunt. It was shot from the second level of the stage out into the audience.

Many believe she captured an entity standing underneath the balcony next to the peanut gallery.

The most famous photo taken at the Ghostlight Theatre!

This photo was captured on an analog camera (one of four cameras running in the theatre that night and the only one to catch something... unusual) during a 2004 performance of *A Christmas Carol*.

In the scene, the ghost of Jacob Marley (played by Jesse Swartz) visits Ebenezer Scrooge (played by Don

Swartz) to warn him of his doomed fate. But if you look closely, there is a third figure on stage, standing directly behind Marley in the corner of the set.

Jesse didn't feel anything—positive or negative—standing behind him when this photo was taken.

Some people see a devil face when looking at the image. Others see something much older. According to German folklore, the Green Man is said to protect old German churches. The Green Man is described as "a horned man peering out from a mask of foliage." Could this horned figure be the church's Green Man? Or is it just another ghost?

No matter what it may be, it was an early indicator that something otherworldly might be hiding out at the Ghostlight Theatre, just waiting for its moment in the spotlight!

Experience the Ghosts of the Ghostlight for Yourself!

Beginning in the 2020/2021 season, the Ghostlight Theatre will start to hold public ghost hunts at the theatre! Whether you are simply curious about the ghost stories or an established paranormal investigator, you are welcome at the Ghostlight!

Ghost hunts will be held in the spring, summer, fall, and winter. They are limited to 30 people and will grant you access to places generally only open to the cast and crew.

Check your program for upcoming dates and how you can get tickets before they sell out!

Appreciation

A book encompassing 20 years of ghost stories would not be possible without the help of cast, crew, and audience members both past and present. Thank you to everyone who contributed their stories to help keep the Ghostlight burning bright!

Allie Schnackel
Ariana Rose
Barb Fronczak
Carla Kwasniak
Carolyn Woomer
Carter Converse
Courtney Gerou
Danny MacKay
Don Swartz
Erica Schrimmel Bazzell
Erin Clare McKay
Gary Cox
Greg Hennessy
Jennifer McFarland
Jesse Swartz
Jill Anderson
Joan Kantor Holesko
Joann Mis
"Joe"
Joe Pieri
Joy Ann Wrona
Julie Senko
Justine Clark Fritz

Justine Swartz
Kathy Ellis Donner
Liz Sanderson
Mallory Allen
Meagan Swartz
Megan Blarr Chapman
Nathan Schuh
Paul McGinnis
Robert Tomasini
Sara Jo
Sarah Fronczak Taravella
Scott Schultz
Sean Polen
Soul Seekers United
Steph Wiechec Luss
Stephanie Harper
Sue Ellen Samuels
Tanya Flynt
Tim Shaw
Tommy Vane
Trey Wydysh
Vanessa Stipkovits

Meet the Owner

L. Don Swartz has been the Artistic/Executive Director at the Ghostlight Theatre since 2001. Prior to that, he was the Artistic/Executive Director of the Ghostlight Theatre Company since 1982. Don has a BA in Theatre Education from Concordia University Chicago and a MAH in Theatre and English from SUNY at Buffalo.

As a playwright, he has 30 published titles that have been produced in nine countries. His titles include *All Through the Night, Noodles, The Birds That Stay, A Night of Dark Intent*, and *The Silver Lady*.

He loves Halloween and is thrilled to be working in a haunted theatre.

Don is the proud father to Emily, Rosie, DJ, and Mikey and loves spending time with his cat, Daisy Mae!

About the Author

Writer, anthropologist, and former international English teacher, Amanda R. Woomer was born and raised in Buffalo, NY. She has been a member of the Ghostlight Theatre since 2005 and has appeared in numerous roles including Madge in *Picnic* (2008), Ado Annie in *Oklahoma!* (2011), Helen in *The Spiral Staircase* (2012), Nell in *All Through the Night* (2015), Ellen in *Noodles* (2017), Daisy in *The Lodger* (2019), and Mina in *Nosferatu* (2020).

She is the owner of Spook-Eats and has written *A Haunted Atlas of Western New York*, *The Spirit Guide: America's Haunted Breweries, Distilleries, and Wineries*, as well as two books in the *Creepy Books for Creepy Kids* series. Follow her spooky adventures at spookeats.com.

Made in the USA
Monee, IL
13 November 2020